I0755946

FINISHING LINE PRESS
www.finishinglinepress.com

Keep Your Damn Seat

poems by

Caroline Kane Kenna

Finishing Line Press
Georgetown, Kentucky

Keep Your Damn Seat

ISBN 979-8-89990-406-6 First Edition

ACKNOWLEDGMENTS

"Jumble," "Dry Summer," and "The Moon Follows the Sun" have appeared in *Kakalak* anthologies

Publisher: Leah Huete de Maines
Editor: Christen Kincaid
Cover Art: Chris Arvidson's "Little Birds"
Author Photo: Elizabeth Ouzts
Cover Design: Elizabeth Maines McCleavy

Order online: www.finishinglinepress.com
also available on amazon.com

Author inquiries and mail orders:
Finishing Line Press
PO Box 1626
Georgetown, Kentucky 40324
USA

Contents

For Patrick, Mark and Logan: staying home with you three gave me fodder and time to write. And for Mike my partner and home.

The Moon Follows the Sun

Dancing like Ginger Rogers,
backwards and in high heels, until evening comes.
She rises then
with thrum and strum of frogs and insects, shining
for the wakeful—all wild and domestic creatures below.
There for the graveyard shifts, night owls burning
midnight, the caregivers, and caretakers. Up
with the tenders and menders, up with fussy babies
up for the sick and dying and waiting up with those who fret.

Twelve times in 365 days.
Unless a blue moon
makes it 13, paper-thin in daylight
and beginning in twilight again.
Growing more with each turn
from new moon with the old in her arms.
A slight wink—a smile in the sky—a crescent charm
the sleepless worry, wishing for dreams
a quarter, half and full she spills over the crown of the mountain
illuminating the corners of home.

Travelogue

…home follows wherever we go, he me and the dog, Our rig
towed behind a big ass truck. I ride, Mike drives.
Point of his elbow rests against the door, hands
11 and 4, steering that Antimatter Blue Ford

long bed, diesel, pick-up, built to Mike's specs pulls
our fifth-wheel camper—not the carbon footprint I envisioned
for going before time notices and tries to catch up, but
how we roll now. I'm second eyes, hands to park, open up

Guinness, prone in the backseat, not even a doggie
side-glance for us. He's silent as a plastic dashboard Jesus,
tongue like the tassel on the Singapore-taxi, good luck cat
charm that hung last on my mom-van mirror.

A big box, it's true, truck and shapeshifting camper together
stretches 50 feet.
Not the Shasta or pop-up of my youth, Mike's single-man tent
or tents we backpacked into Grand Canyon.
The night the Milky Way spilled stars like dice in a game
of celestial Yahtzee while our boys snored.

In truth, it's not my crone-age dream, that two-seater
English country romp is late-night campfire conversation
script still in development as we rage on
here, in the RV now.

Dreaming is solitary, making it real takes two,
roadster later, maybe, I'll drive. This travelogue, tripping along
together wherever we tie up next.

Jumble

After Michele Hoffman's Walk the Line

Tiny sandals, soft soles maybe
babies' shoes handed down, outgrown
before the next could lace up.
This crowded assemblage glowing red
takes me back to sweet feet
across my palm. I measured three
pair with thumb and forefinger
while they nursed.

Once little piggies gobbled, tender
toes learning to walk in red clay
and midwestern mud:

The Land of One Lost Shoe
and dirty socks, shooting hoops
in the driveway, running
around neighborhoods; sweaty,
stinky after baseball games
and soccer practice. Rollerblades,
pads and helmets in the cul-de-sac plastic
hockey sticks, red like those shoes
hanging on the gallery wall. Memories
by the basket full kept at the door.
The boys' flips, tennis shoes, cleats, now
men's dress browns, wingtips
on the threshold.

Coming Soon

For Miss Lentil

In January, the Flowering Apricot
in the backyard blooms pink all over. The first
tree of spring, a gift your parents gave us,
pops of pink all over. I think of you,

how balloon-like buds on your parents' tree
are the shape of your tiny fists and toes
in sonograms shared. First grand
twinkle to Lentil,
the Future Voters sticker
on your Mom's belly. First girl
by Christmas, baby bump size of a coconut,
a cauliflower head on Groundhog Day
on Groundhog Day…an acorn squash on and on
as they and we prepare for your May arrival.

By then Miss Lentil, the Ornamental
Apricot will have traded petals for leaves
little bitty fruits dangling from its branches,
will dance with the bees. And we will rock
and sing, and I'll measure your feet
with thumb and forefinger like I did for
your Dad when he was a baby, too.

Concerning This 1928 *New Yorker* Review

"The House at Pooh Corner, made me want to throw up"
Dorothy Parker

Dear Dorothy,
For a time, I wanted to be you—practiced puns like a Shakespearean
actor auditioning swords—perfecting parry, thrust, why I even tried
swilling gin; but this is about you sticking it to
Winnie the Pooh.

That moronic swipe at A. A. Milne's debut rattles,
demands I defend the bear, our books. Truth is,
Dorothy, you get the last laugh, I won't go into the Milne
saga or how sweet, storied Winnie, was Mickey's foil long
before copyright expired; a horror star now, yes, really.

What's more, I don't know if this is riff or chorus
moron, Mama's late-in-life word not my go-to. She was the one
who snuggled us close, the bedtime reader bringing that world
of tender tales alive as we turned pages; later she tucked
grandsons in with those bear tales. I'll hear her voice again
when I read Pooh to my grands, too. Do these

sugar-coated lines make you gag, Dorothy? I'm sorry
you had no reading mother; that you shed silly and kind
like a dry umbilical stump, grew fangs as first teeth. I do see
how that world could be too-bloody sweet for a door-kicker
like you, brightest wit at the Algonquin table, the sharpest-tongue,
but
tut-tut Dorothy, everybody, yes even you, needs a little honey
and love from this silly ole bear, his pals too, so there!

Warmly,
A 21st century grandmother, on behalf of her mother and
Winnie the Pooh.

Moving Parts

After Jody Lynn's Life Journeys

A Hula-Hoop circles hips.
Legs straight, feet on surface,
rim, toes pointed leaping
across space-time.
Hair flying, racing through
skating on.

The motion
catches the eyes
of angels charged with
minding balance, juggling
orbits as the planet spins.
Listening for hints of danger,
slightest change in hum.
A whiff of smoke or shift
in the earth's crust
clattering plates.

I only know you in pictures

After Van Gogh's La Berceuse, Portrait of Madame Roulin

In these still model hands, I see the grandmother
I only know in pictures and stories my Dad and the aunts
told that I retell now.

Jessamine of Kentucky claimed Kansas as home.
Recovered health out west like Teddy Roosevelt.
She rode a mule on Grand Canyon's Bright
Angel Trail. A principal

elementary school trailblazer, Dad said
and like women then, tending children, making
rationing victory while preparing her own to wed,
to serve, she had to sign Dad's WW 2 enlistment papers.

Kin to King Robert the Bruce but every good
blue-faced, Scots-Irish, claims him. A suffragist
marching in a photo. The fiery pen defending
a daughter, spoon that served squirrel stew
on fancy luncheon plates to Fanny and Edna.

Wife of the life of the party. Newly wedded
when he moved his mother in and then out, she
made him choose. Her movie-star handsome, cad
of a husband called her Nin—short for ninny.
After she lost her voice, she cut her eyes, clicked
her tongue, pointed a finger at grandfather
and at her nurse. Dad declared, "my mother was no fool."

This Van Gogh is the last picture in our family album.
It's a blurry, black-n-white candid he snapped
Grandmother Jessamine is rising from a lawn chair.
She glares at him and stares at me now
daring me to flesh her out.

I'm Lucky

Supine, I close my left eye,
right cheek is numb, bare.
A sterile drape
mutes the too-bright light
above the chair, strains of Bob
Marley's "*don't worry 'bout a 'ting*"
drifting by. In my mind, I sing
It's a good thing I have
chipmunk cheeks.
I'm lucky I know.

I could blame my Scots Irish make up, freckle-faced
love of sun, summers in the suntan, baby oil,
iodine years.
I'm lucky I know.

The surgeon
paints half my potato face, something cold,
something smelly-clean and begins cutting
rooting out skin deep cancer—layer
by layer. I see him as a strip-miner
clean before the shift covers him in dust, soot.
The light on his head moves as he removes a mountain,
piece by piece. Pressure, not pain. All clear.
Big scar, my mirror says,
I'm lucky I know.

The heat whooshes from a vent
above the door, matching my relief,
I'm lucky I know.

To keep myself from touching that drape
while he sews 40 stitches to close,
I squeeze arm rests, wiggle fingers, make circles
in the air with pointed toes. Antsy
my reply when the surgeon stops mid-seam,

asks if I'm okay. I close my eyes,
          I'm lucky I know.

Under this drape, I am,
a bare cheek—stitching yet to finish.
A faceless Rene Magritte. Lava
lamp churning green, red, purple
behind fluttering lids. Word soundings
sounding better on the stage in my head
than on this page as I wait for bruises to heal
sutures to come out and to reveal the next face
my mirror and I will have to grow into.
          I'm lucky I know.

Keep Your Damn Seat

Once I was the girl with a strawberry curl
in the middle of her forehead. First daughter *very,*
very good and horrid at times.

Twice, I've swallowed hell before sputtering no
when asked if I was mother to Kenna men
older than I am. What the fuck…I swear

I heard my brother-in-law laughing
laughing his ass off in the narthex before the priest
celebrated his life and blessed his ashes, the joke
could have been Jim's. I shoulda

cracked back or fixed the guy with my steely
blue Mama-stare countering his with my
only *if there's immaculate conception in the womb*
genius that never crosses my lips…again,

A med-tech, millennial, this time, asked if my husband
was my son. It was after I smiled like Heath Ledger's
why-so-serious-Joker and a PA had inked a scalpel
template, but before my cheek was numbed.

Q-Tips, my copper-haired oldest son, Patrick's
code for the sunbaked state. Old bones, old eyes
snowbirds still casting shadows.
Why did I go there? Oh yeah, that seat
I won't be labeled, patronized or boxed with a bow
lumped into categories and stats. Senior happiness scales
brace yourselves….

Broken down while traveling

The stone skipped across space-time
willy nilly, carrying the alchemy
of stars long gone. It spins on and off
comet tails losing and gathering
elements and size before igniting
in Earth's atmosphere. A moon's moon
burnt to a nub that sticks
in the horizon's eye like pollen.
Accidental satellite, turning last leaf,
of a precious plant, poked into fresh dirt,
new roots, new seed the Earth tows
until it drops from orbit, catching
another current, the next ride.

On Your Way Home

In memory of Tom, heart of the Kane order, 1963-2025,
baseball was life and a language we share

Hey little brother, when your flagging Orioles beat
my surging Cardinals, I could almost hear
you whisper, yes, see you pump your fist
at every wicked pitch and double play. Your offense
was swinging and your outfielders had wheels,
their mitts up like your ears. I confess I followed
the series on my phone couldn't bear the static,

dear brother, those TV talkers are but flickers, empty
heads, glints in a colorless den without your recollection
of parks, pitchers' stories and batters' stats. Nothing
beats your eye roll defense of umps & refs, or that little shake
of your head when I gush over my players
like a little league Mom. Besides bro, if I had tuned in

I might've glimpsed you in that hometown wave, circling
bases. You, messing with my birds' bats, dressed like you did
in the years we traveled and cheered together,
no need for tickets. Looking back over those times I see

you in Baltimore for Cal and Boog, long balls, Earl Weaver
hot after a mistake or a run-down cost his Os the lead,
smoke and barbecue drifting Camden Yard summer seats
and the last bleachers in spring rain. We high-fived a sweep,
sang *Take Me Out to the Ballgame* 'til breathless as we'd done
in Baltimores past, with nephews in strollers, at your knees
your elbows. In Atlanta, Chicago, and in St. Louis,

Busch Stadium. Homer's landing and nosebleed sections. Thrilling
seasons, and walk-off wins. Counting strikes, balls, sticky
plastic hats, melty *Dippin' Dots*. There for hot dogs,
cold beer, as Redbirds broke records, for air swings
those trips you made to us seemed easy

even when they weren't. The annual family sing-along
last swing. The stretch, the slide
root root root for the Cardinals. Little pieces
of major league happiness. I'll carry that 7th inning song
until we meet again, Tom, *at the old ballgame.*

Lake-scape

The coy fish goes deep
to avoid sunburn. An osprey
shatters the morning,
its gray wings charting cloud
heights, circling construction raw,
red, and old clay scars.
Keening at shadows' reach,
the bird touches
down in a wall of trees,
folds like leaves. Amber eyes
shifting from the beach
to the cove's mouth. As a fish
breaks the quiet water,
osprey dives, rising with a flash
of silver in its claws.

Time Is Wasting

After Dali's Persistence of Memory

Dead bees'
faces and the dance of clocks.
The shelf life of honey more than ours. Are these
bones, ants and flies this painter's vision of a planet
too hot for glacier or grass? His spare brush
leafless branches, no birds, no butterflies.

Do the math—the clock ticks ever closer
to midnight as warning and challenge to us
humans who inherited the Post Eden Pact.
Blue sky, free rein, seeds for gardens, family trees,
in exchange for tending planet needs, but

when we chose smoke, wheels we broke the deal
and started our own clock. Advancing hands
again and again ignoring the clock painter's
waking dream, poets' lines, the prophets'
signs and Einstein's projections on lifespan
numbers, pollinators, get the drift?
Arithmetic meant to reel everyone in,
ginned up debate instead. All while colony
collapse continues and Dali's shadow deepens.

Global sweat, Arctic to Antarctica shedding raises
tides. Hot, red waves of algae, angry sharks in toxic seas
peril for fish and our grandchildren. No wonder
whales are beaching themselves. Yet, I still believe
we humans are Earth's best hope unless
the last bee dies.

Dry Summer

A striped umbrella shades the makeshift tomato stand. The table piled with stop sign colors invites me to pull in, park. Carolina's go-to for home-grown fruit, Roy Caldwell, sits in the back of a pickup under the carport. His legs stirring this July heat. White buckets of tomatoes in the truck bed surround him like grandchildren.

"If the umbrella is open, so I am," he says ambling toward the shady side of the table.
His cane in one hand, bucket in the other, as I finger the harvest. Lose myself in visions of recipes, tomato-cucumber salad with a French vinaigrette, my mother-in-law's sweet tomato conserve, the best B.L.T., Sandra's tomato pie and that spicy gazpacho I'm dying to try.

Mama taught me how to preserve in Mason jars. The ripest peel easily, blanch for end-of-garden
soups, her bounty lined the winter pantry like red jellyfish in amber.
"I'd given up hope for good tomatoes this year," my reply.

Caldwell smiles a toothless smile, tilts his cap off his forehead. I can see his eyes and he can see mine. "I'm 91, retired 25 years ago, started farming at 14 behind a mule and plow. These tomato vines all I got now." He's culling as we talk, the slightly squishy, bruised, split-skins—white start of rot—from the small red but perfect tabletop treasure. "They're not producing like they use'ta. I might be done." He pokes at the pile with his cane, apologies for the size while

I weigh my selection, take a few more, weigh again and hand him money. "This is a first, we didn't grow our own this year and I've been craving these". Bagging up produce I add, "size doesn't matter for pizza sauce; besides, it's been a weird growing year. Too wet, tomatoes don't set blossoms. When it's this hot, they won't set fruit."

Caldwell chucks rot in the plastic bucket, "I don't know about climate change, but I do know tomatoes, and this is all I got."

Murmurations

For Nancy, "Think of me as something with wings"

After you passed away,
you were a wren and the Red-Shouldered Hawk
catching breath in a Crepe Myrtle, leaving
lilac-colored blossoms behind and Florida cranes

graceful on gray-white wings, kites
above St. Lucie's Inlet and the gawky pair squawking
at the dog behind our camper. Those birds perhaps like us
walking at dusk calling our boys home for dinner.

What I know about cranes
I learned from your feathery-soft retelling
of you and your Greg, watching Sandhill cranes
migrating, 20,000 wings landing, taking off…

When husband Mike and I glimpse those Savannas kin,
They mate for life, I say to him.

Truth is, you are a dragonfly too. Your last
words summoned again by this one suspended
feet from my nose, four iridescent wings,
two-pair blurring air. Is that you zipping through?

Yet to be

When I see you
in the April sonogram you are
chubby cheeks, pouty lip, unseeing eyes
pressed to a window nearest
your mother's heart. 3-D Study
Sweet Baby Girl in Utero Eight Months,
face of the future, the bust or a portrait
of waiting in the family museum
pushing boundaries already. Curled like Alice

in her cat condo and Kona dog at the door
ready to bolt when the glass slides open a crack.
Familiar now with your mother's heart,
her beats, your father's gentle tone,
the next best thing, until May
when you shed bean state and become Sylvie Rae.

Thick dark hair, your Mama's nose, your Dad's
long fingers and witchy toes. First girl
after raising your dad, your uncles. First grand
perfect rosebud on this branch. Pink face,
pink lips puckered. Daddy's pride, Mom's joyful
work, so sleepy when we meet, I cradle, sing
your tiny fist keeping time.

The Moon Follows the Sun (reprise)

...Twelve times in 365 days. Unless, a blue moon makes it 13,
paper-thin in daylight and beginning in twilight again. Growing
more with each turn from new moon with the old in her arms.

A slight wink—a smile in the sky—crescent
charm, the sleepless worry wishing for dreams....

With Thanks

Here goes…family and friends, the voices I hear when I write and the ones here, now reminding me how fast time goes. The poets' villages that help me discover, refine and shape my poems: The Friday zoomers, The Charlotte Writers Club critique groups. Open mics, online poets' mentorship and the Wildacres "nation" at The Table Rock Writers Conference.

Caroline Kane Kenna was born in Missouri and grew up in mountains of Viginia. Daughter of book and puzzle lovers who were active in the church and community, her father was the local newspaper editor and her mother, an English scholar, volunteer tutor and a quilter. They encouraged their four children to bloom where they were planted. Gathering news for the weekly was part of family life and how to give back, supper conversation. After college, Caroline worked for her dad before taking reporting jobs in Culpeper where she met her husband Mike and his career took the family to the Midwest. While a trailing spouse and stay at home Mom for three boys, she drafted several novels, wrote memoir and volunteered at church and in her sons' schools. She found poetry and her people in the Carolinas.

Her poems have placed in Charlotte Writers Club contests, are published in *Kakalak* anthologies and in *Above the Fold* (*Main Street Rag*), North Carolina Poetry Society's Poetry in Plain Sight and in ekphrastic exhibits at Queen City Art. Her essays appear in anthologies: *Foolhardy*, (Personal Story Publishing Project), *For the Love of Baseball (McFarland) and Reflections on the New River* (McFarland). She attends Table Rock Writers Conference, is a poet of "the free nation of Shabazz" and frequents open mics in the Charlotte area. A former president of Charlotte Writers Club and a member of the board of directors. She holds B.A. from King College and a B.A. from Memphis State. *Keep Your Damn Seat* is her first chapbook.

www.ingramcontent.com/pod-product-compliance
Lightning Source LLC
LaVergne TN
LVHW090542110826
845146LV00003B/1237